SUPERHEROES OF SCIENCE

RACHEL CARSON

ENVIRONMENTAL CRUSADER

Nancy Dickmann

Gareth Stevens
PUBLISHING

Please visit our website, **www.garethstevens.com**. For a free color catalog of all our high-quality books, call toll free 1-800-542-2595 or fax 1-877-542-2596.

Library of Congress Cataloging-in-Publication Data
Dickmann, Nancy.
Rachel Carson: environmental crusader / by Nancy Dickmann.
p. cm. – (Superheroes of science)
Includes index.
ISBN 978-1-4824-3149-0 (pbk.)
ISBN 978-1-4824-3152-0 (6 pack)
ISBN 978-1-4824-3150-6 (library binding)
1. Carson, Rachel, – 1907-1964 – Juvenile literature.
2. Biologists – United States – Biography – Juvenile literature. 3. Environmentalists – United States – Biography – Juvenile literature. I. Dickmann, Nancy. II. Title.
QH31.C33 D53 2016
333.95'16092–d23

Published in 2016 by
Gareth Stevens Publishing
111 East 14th Street, Suite 349
New York, NY 10003

Produced for Gareth Stevens by Calcium
Editors for Calcium: 3REDCARS
Designers: Paul Myerscough and 3REDCARS

Picture credits: Cover art by Mat Edwards; Dreamstime: Ken Cole 12b, Erashov 24c, Lorrainehudgins 15t, Ivan Mikhaylov 18c, Snehitdesign 7t, Teri Virbickis 43t; Shutterstock: Allan Wood Photography 25t, Anest 39t, Blueeyes 11c, Darren J. Bradley 17c, B Brown 33t, Catwalker 45b, Ded Pixto 28t, HD1 Photography 27t, Kan Khampanya 9t, Rocky33 5t, Martynova Anna 31t, Psamtik 32b, Mike Truchon 36b, Vilainecrevette 16c, Xuanlu Wang 35t; Wikimedia Commons: 21b, 26b, 44c, Jeremy Atherton 21t, Library of Congress 29b, 40b, OSU Special Collections & Archives 37c, Project Gutenberg 6c, US Department of Agriculture 13t, US Fish and Wildlife Service 5c, 23c, White House Press Office 41c.

Printed in the United States of America
CPSIA compliance information: Batch #CS15GS: For further information contact Gareth Stevens, New York, New York at 1-800-542-2595.

CONTENTS

Chapter 1

WHO WAS RACHEL CARSON?

One day early in 1958, Olga Owens Huckins sat down at her desk to write a letter. She was furious. She and her husband lived on the Massachusetts coast, where they had a bird sanctuary. Over the past year, state and federal agencies had repeatedly sprayed the ground to destroy mosquitoes, using airplanes to spread synthetic pesticides over a large area. As a result, many birds had died, and their habitat had been contaminated with dangerous chemicals. Why, she wondered, was nothing being done to stop this poisoning?

Huckins was writing to her friend, Rachel Carson. Carson had trained as a biologist, but she was now an author, famous for her books and articles on nature, especially sea life. She had a gift of writing about nature in a poetic, inspiring way. Huckins hoped

SUPERHERO STAT

War on Insects

Spraying with pesticides was common in the 1950s. State and federal agencies were trying to control insects such as fire ants, gypsy moths, and mosquitoes, which could harm crops or spread disease. In 1956, a program to spray more than 3,000,000 acres (1,200,000 ha) across ten states began. During the summer of 1957, one area of Long Island was sprayed 14 times in a single day!

In the 1950s, pesticides were thought to be the best way to combat insects that destroyed crops and other plants.

Carson won praise for her ability to explain difficult science concepts to the general public.

that Carson might be able to write something that would bring the issue to the public's attention.

Carson had already been interested in the subject of pesticides. For years, she had been aware of the evidence that was slowly mounting up, showing that pesticides were having an effect on wildlife, as well as on human health. She agreed with Huckins that something had to be done. Over the next few years, she carefully gathered data and worked on a book.

When that book, *Silent Spring*, was published in 1962, it had the force of a bomb. Suddenly people were demanding answers from the government. Why, they asked, were these agencies allowed to poison the land, and the people and animals living on it? Carson had opened up a debate whose effects are still being felt today.

EARLY LIFE

Rachel Louise Carson was born on May 27, 1907, in the small Pennsylvania town of Springdale. Her father, Robert Carson, was an insurance salesman, the son of Irish immigrants. Her mother, Maria, came from an old Pennsylvania family. Rachel had two older siblings—Marian and Robert.

The Carsons were a close family, but they were poor. Their four-room house had no central heating or indoor plumbing, and enough electricity only for ceiling lights. However, although their house was small, the family had 64 acres (26 ha) of land, which was a wonderful space for the children to play and learn about the natural world. The land contained an orchard of apple and pear trees, a vegetable garden, and a chicken coop, and the Allegheny River was not far away.

Maria Carson had been a teacher before her marriage. She liked to read and to help her children learn, and one of the most important things she passed on to them was a love of nature. She enjoyed studying plants, bird-watching, and exploring the

THE TALE OF MR. JEREMY FISHER

BY BEATRIX POTTER

As a young girl, Carson loved reading stories by Beatrix Potter, who wrote about the adventures of animals such as Peter Rabbit and Jeremy Fisher.

The Allegheny River runs through the hilly woodlands of western Pennsylvania, near the Carson family home, before joining with the Monongahela River to form the Ohio River.

SUPERHERO FACT

Two Great Passions

Carson always knew what she wanted to be. At a talk she gave in 1954, Carson said, "I can remember no time, even in earliest childhood, when I didn't assume I was going to be a writer. Also, I can remember no time when I wasn't interested in the out-of-doors and the whole world of nature."

woods and the wildlife along the Allegheny River. Rachel grew up spending as much time as possible outside, learning about nature.

Rachel's other main interests were reading and writing. She loved stories about animals, such as tales by the British writer and naturalist Beatrix Potter, and *The Wind in the Willows* by Kenneth Grahame, another British author. As soon as Rachel could write, she began to compose her own stories about animals and nature. When she was just ten years old, she submitted a story to one of her favorite magazines and was delighted when it was published. Her career as a writer was off to a great start!

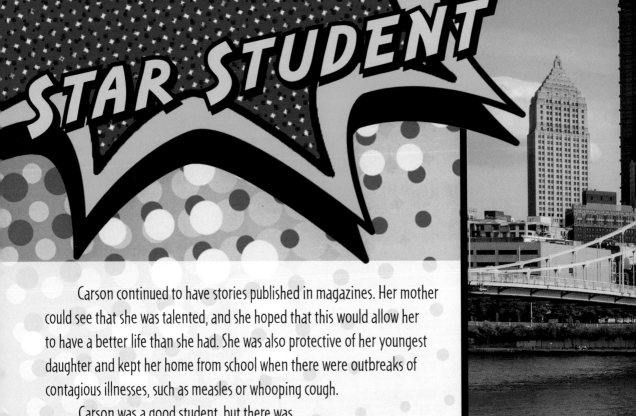

Carson continued to have stories published in magazines. Her mother could see that she was talented, and she hoped that this would allow her to have a better life than she had. She was also protective of her youngest daughter and kept her home from school when there were outbreaks of contagious illnesses, such as measles or whooping cough.

Carson was a good student, but there was no high school in her town. Some students took the train to a nearby high school, but the Carsons could not afford the fare. For the first two years of high school, Carson took lessons at home and in the town. Finally, in eleventh grade, she was able to go to high school a few miles away in Parnassus, traveling back and forth on the trolley. She graduated in 1925 at the top of her class.

Carson won admission to the Pennsylvania College for Women (PCW, now Chatham University), located in Pittsburgh, about 16 miles (26 km)

Carson traveled to high school on a trolley like this one.

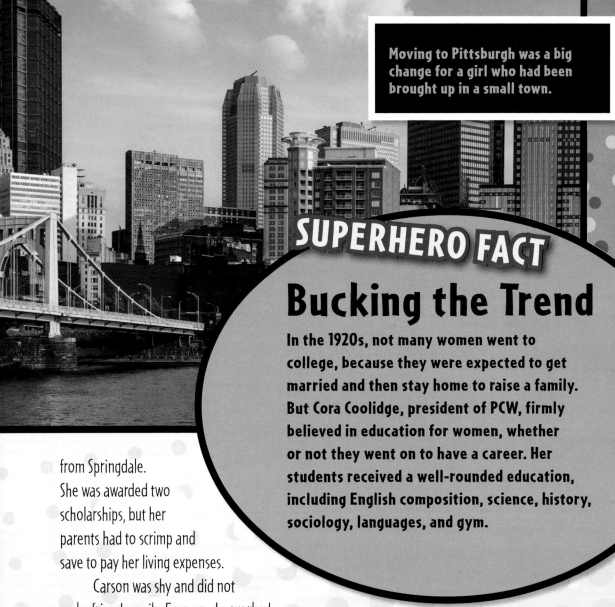

Moving to Pittsburgh was a big change for a girl who had been brought up in a small town.

SUPERHERO FACT

Bucking the Trend

In the 1920s, not many women went to college, because they were expected to get married and then stay home to raise a family. But Cora Coolidge, president of PCW, firmly believed in education for women, whether or not they went on to have a career. Her students received a well-rounded education, including English composition, science, history, sociology, languages, and gym.

from Springdale. She was awarded two scholarships, but her parents had to scrimp and save to pay her living expenses.

Carson was shy and did not make friends easily. Even so, she worked hard in her classes and also took part in other activities, such as basketball and field hockey. She had entered PCW as an English major, but after taking a biology class, her teacher saw her potential and eventually persuaded her to switch to biology. It was a good choice—Carson enjoyed her new classes and did so well that when she graduated in 1929 it was as only one of three students to achieve *magna cum laude*.

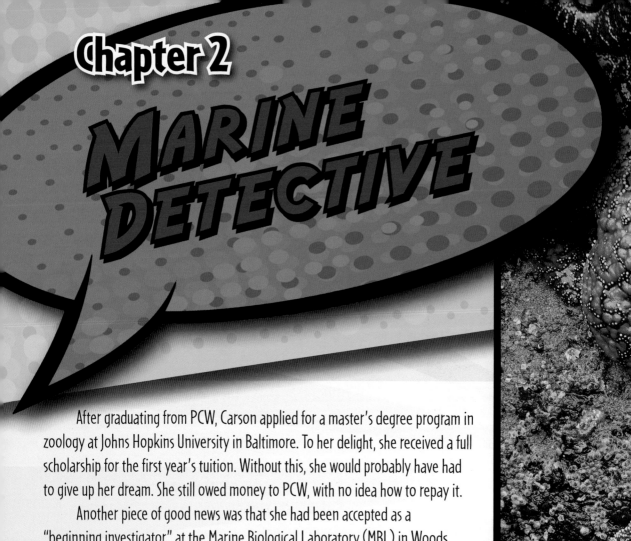

Chapter 2

MARINE DETECTIVE

After graduating from PCW, Carson applied for a master's degree program in zoology at Johns Hopkins University in Baltimore. To her delight, she received a full scholarship for the first year's tuition. Without this, she would probably have had to give up her dream. She still owed money to PCW, with no idea how to repay it.

Another piece of good news was that she had been accepted as a "beginning investigator" at the Marine Biological Laboratory (MBL) in Woods Hole, Massachusetts. Before starting at Johns Hopkins, Carson would spend eight weeks studying invertebrates. It was an incredible experience for her, and one that allowed her to explore tide pools and examine live animals in their natural habitats, instead of preserved specimens in jars.

At Johns Hopkins Carson loved her classes and her lab work but found it difficult to be so far from home. She had no extra money to travel back to visit her family. She began looking for a house to rent and convinced her parents to move down to Baltimore. However, she was still having money troubles, and in

Wow!

Many sea creatures, including these sea stars, are invertebrates. This means that they do not have a backbone like humans do.

Magnet for Super-scientists

As many as 55 Nobel Prize-winning scientists have worked with MBL, which was founded in 1888 as a center for research and education in biology. Each year, its 300-strong staff are joined by more than 300 visiting scientists and young researchers from around the world, as well as faculty and students. MBL's location on the Massachusetts coast makes it a perfect place to learn about coastal ecosystems.

her second year she had to look for a job and become a part-time student. She soon found work in a laboratory, researching the genetics of rats and fruit flies.

Carson finished her master's degree in 1932 and spent another happy summer carrying out research at the MBL in Woods Hole. She then went back to Johns Hopkins to begin her PhD in zoology. However, money was still a problem, and her father and sister were both in poor health and unable to work. With a heavy heart, Rachel–the most able and reliable of the Carson children–had to give up her studies to support her family.

FINDING HER WAY

Carson was at a crossroads in her life. She had started teaching biology at the University of Maryland Dental School while still a master's student, and she continued to do that. In the meantime, she started looking for a full-time college teaching position, but she knew it would be hard to find one without a PhD.

Since switching her major from English to biology, Carson had more or less stopped writing. Now it seemed a possible source of income. She sent some of her best college work off to magazines, but all of it was rejected. Instead of giving up, she worked hard on revising it to try again, and found to her delight that her love of writing was reawakened.

In 1935, Carson's father died suddenly. She now had to support not only herself but also her mother, her sister, who had left her husband, and her sister's two young daughters. She turned for help to her old friend Mary Scott Skinker, who had been her biology teacher at PCW. Skinker was a full-time zoology researcher for the Department of Agriculture. She encouraged Carson to prepare for the exams that would qualify her for a government position.

In the days before television, many people listened to radio programs instead. Writing the scripts for these programs, as Carson did, was an important job.

Top Marks

Carson worked hard with Mary Scott Skinker to prepare for the civil service exams. She scored 61 points in the exam for wildlife biologists, 75 points in the exam for aquatic biologists, and 76.5 points in the parasitology exam. She outscored all other applicants and later became only the second woman ever to be hired by the US Bureau of Fisheries.

When Carson began teaching at the University of Maryland's dental school, she was the only female biology teacher on the staff.

If teaching work was unavailable, working for the government might be a good option. Skinker introduced Carson to Elmer Higgins, director of the US Bureau of Fisheries. His department was producing a series of short radio programs on marine life, and he needed someone to write the scripts. With her writing and science experience, Carson was the perfect person for the job.

NATURE WRITER

For the next eight months, Carson wrote scripts for the radio program *Romance Under the Waters*. She had a natural gift for making the science material interesting and easy for the general public to understand. Elmer Higgins liked what she wrote, and so did his superiors. When the series was finished, he asked her to write an introduction to marine life that would be published as a government brochure.

Carson started work on the essay, which she planned to call "World of Waters." At the same time, she used the research for her radio scripts to write several feature articles on the marine life of Chesapeake Bay, the large inlet bordered by

STAR CONTRIBUTION

Super Communicator

Thanks to her talents as a writer, Carson was able to reach people who might not otherwise have been interested in science or nature. Her articles opened people's eyes to the problems and challenges facing the natural world, and introduced many people to the concept of conservation.

Ouch!

The shad—here caught in the mouth of a heron—is a fish related to the herring. It lives in the Chesapeake Bay and many other places. One of Carson's first successful articles was about shad fishing in Chesapeake Bay.

Maryland and Virginia on the Atlantic coast. She had some success with this, although her articles appeared under the name "R. L. Carson." She and her editors thought that her work would be taken more seriously if people did not realize a woman had written it.

In April 1936, Carson gave Higgins the text for her brochure, but he thought it was too good for a government pamphlet. He urged her to submit it to the *Atlantic Monthly*, a prestigious magazine. Before long, she was offered a permanent job with the Bureau of Fisheries. As a junior aquatic biologist, she would be analyzing data about fish populations, writing reports, and drafting brochures for the public. She liked the work, and the regular income was a huge help to her family.

Chapter 3

SEA LIFE EXPLORER

By the end of 1936, Carson's writings for magazines were going well. She had more articles published, and she gradually built up a network of useful contacts, including editors, scientists, and fishermen. However, more troubles were ahead. In January 1937, Carson's sister Marian died of pneumonia. Although her mother took care of Marian's two daughters and acted as housekeeper, Carson was now the sole breadwinner of the family, a position she found very stressful. To save money, the family moved to a different house, in Silver Spring, Maryland. It was closer to Carson's work, and near good schools for the girls, but it was farther from the forests and the bay that she loved so much.

Carson decided to try to sell "World of Waters," the essay she had written for the government brochure. The *Atlantic Monthly* loved the article and agreed to publish it with a new title—"Undersea." In it Carson had described life under the oceans, as though the reader were on a guided submarine tour. After it was published, she received a letter from Quincy Howe, an editor at

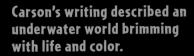

Carson's writing described an underwater world brimming with life and color.

Super-keen Observer

Carson loved doing field research, talking to fishermen and other scientists as well as observing nature. She always carried a small spiral notebook with her, and typed up her notes at home on index cards, stored in a wooden box on her desk.

The "Undersea" article written by Carson showed readers the wonders of life on the ocean floor.

a New York publishing house. Had Carson, he asked, ever thought about writing a book on this topic?

After meeting with Howe, Carson developed a plan for not one, but three books. One would cover coastal life, one would look at life in the open ocean, and the last would explore the deepest parts of the sea. She began writing, but she still had to earn a living. While she worked on the book, Carson continued her job at the Bureau of Fisheries, and published more articles in magazines.

SUCCESS AT WORK

Things were finally going well for Carson. Elmer Higgins, her boss at the Bureau of Fisheries, gave her a promotion. He realized what her real talents were, and created a new job for her. She no longer did field research, and cut down on her laboratory work, in order to focus on analyzing data and writing reports.

With everything else going on in her life, Carson found it difficult to find time to work on her book. She wrote early in the morning or late in the evening, when the house was quiet. Whenever she could, she went on research trips. On one trip to Woods Hole she spent hours sitting on the dock, watching the mackerel swim beneath her. In her book, she explored the range of animals that live on the coast, with a focus on seabirds, mackerel, and eels. She outlined each animal's struggle to survive, looking at how the different living things in this ecosystem are dependent on each other. Even after death, an animal's body is broken down and becomes food for the next generation of sea creatures.

Carson's hard work paid off, and when her book *Under the Sea-Wind* was finally published in

Zoom!

Shoals of mackerel migrate up and down the Atlantic coast each year.

Conservation Pioneer

The newspaper and magazine articles that Carson wrote during this time were starting to champion conservation— the need to preserve natural resources and protect nature. She firmly believed that humans caused the decline of wildlife by upsetting the balance of nature, by draining swamps, plowing fields, and cutting down forests.

STAR CONTRIBUTION

November 1941, it received glowing reviews. She was especially pleased to hear scientists as well as editors praising her writing and research. However, the timing was bad. Only a month after the book was published, the Japanese Air Force attacked the US Navy base at Pearl Harbor in Hawaii. As a result, the United States entered World War II, and that dominated the news from then on. People had other things on their minds, and *Under the Sea-Wind* sold only 2,000 copies.

One of the birds featured in *Under the Sea-Wind* is the black skimmer, which feeds on insects and sea creatures.

AWARD-WINNING BOOK

World War II affected more than just book sales—everyone was expected to do their part. Carson qualified as an air raid warden and took an evening class in first aid. She also had to move to Chicago in 1942 when the Bureau of Fisheries relocated. Eventually a job opened up in Washington, and she was able to return to the East Coast. Her new responsibilities, however, left her little time for writing.

Over the next few years, Carson rose through the ranks at the Bureau of Fisheries. Yet, she was unhappy with her job and wanted to be able to support her family by writing full time. She continued to write articles but was reluctant to spend time on a book after the commercial failure of *Under the Sea-Wind*.

In 1948, she decided to seek out an agent to help sell

Pow!

Carson moved briefly to Chicago when her department relocated to the Merchandise Mart building.

SUPERHERO STAT

Global Star

The Sea Around Us stayed on the best-seller list for 86 weeks, with 32 of those weeks at number one. Since its publication, the book has been translated into 28 languages.

her work. She met Marie Rodell, who encouraged her to write another book about sea life. Carson's research for her articles had continually provided her with new material, which she had filed away for future use. She began writing, and in July 1951 *The Sea Around Us* was published. Some of its chapters were also published in magazines, and to Carson's delight her work was chosen for the nationwide Book-of-the-Month book-buying club.

Like Carson, John Burroughs was a nature writer, and a pioneer of the conservation movement. The medal that Carson won was established in his honor.

The book was an immediate success. It got good reviews, and it also sold well. In 1952, it won the National Book Award for Nonfiction. It also won the Burroughs Medal, the prestigious award given by the John Burroughs Association for the best nature book of the year. At last, after all her years of hard work, Carson had become a nationally respected writer.

Chapter 4

INFLUENTIAL AUTHOR

Carson had become an overnight star. She was constantly in demand to sign books, pose for photos, and be interviewed on radio and television. She was a naturally shy person, though, and preferred being outside enjoying nature, or spending time with close friends. However, she realized that this was her chance to make writing her full-time career, so she let Marie Rodell set up a schedule of public appearances.

Public speaking did not come naturally to Carson. As she did with all her work, she prepared carefully, writing and revising each speech, and typing out note cards. She had a quiet voice but also an air of authority that impressed her audiences. As the months went on, she became more confident about speaking out on subjects that interested her. Several influential people, including the daughter of former president Theodore Roosevelt, had read and enjoyed *The Sea Around Us*. Their support helped publicize it even more, so Carson was kept busy.

Although she was now a well-known author, Carson was still happiest exploring nature.

Woman in a Man's World

Part of the public interest in Carson had to do with the fact that she was a woman. In the eyes of most people at the time, science was a job for men. However, she was determined to show that biology was a subject for anyone with a passion for nature. "People often seem to be surprised that a woman has written a book about the sea," she said, in one speech. "This is especially true, I find, of men."

STAR CONTRIBUTION

While Carson traveled around the country to promote the book, Rodell kept busy, too. She sold the rights to translate *The Sea Around Us* into many other languages and made a deal with a studio to make a documentary film based on the book. Carson would review the script and help promote the finished film. All this hard work paid off—the money from the book, magazine, and film deals gave her the financial security to quit her job at the Bureau of Fisheries. Now she could become a full-time writer.

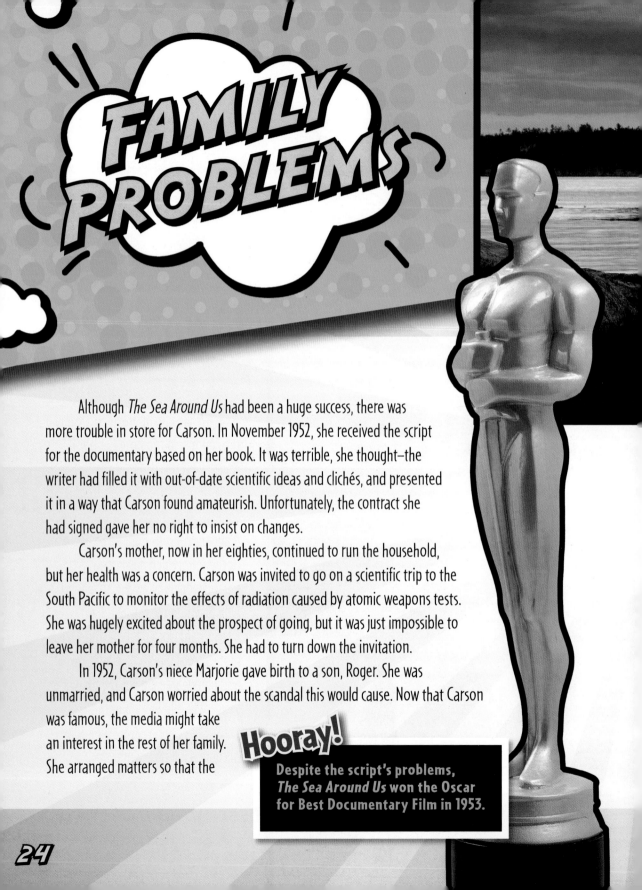

FAMILY PROBLEMS

Although *The Sea Around Us* had been a huge success, there was more trouble in store for Carson. In November 1952, she received the script for the documentary based on her book. It was terrible, she thought–the writer had filled it with out-of-date scientific ideas and clichés, and presented it in a way that Carson found amateurish. Unfortunately, the contract she had signed gave her no right to insist on changes.

Carson's mother, now in her eighties, continued to run the household, but her health was a concern. Carson was invited to go on a scientific trip to the South Pacific to monitor the effects of radiation caused by atomic weapons tests. She was hugely excited about the prospect of going, but it was just impossible to leave her mother for four months. She had to turn down the invitation.

In 1952, Carson's niece Marjorie gave birth to a son, Roger. She was unmarried, and Carson worried about the scandal this would cause. Now that Carson was famous, the media might take an interest in the rest of her family. She arranged matters so that the

Hooray!

Despite the script's problems, *The Sea Around Us* won the Oscar for Best Documentary Film in 1953.

Carson fell in love with the Maine coast and spent as much time as she could there.

Science All Around Us

Carson wanted to show that science was more than just men in lab coats—rather, it was something that affected everyone's lives. In her acceptance speech at the National Book Awards, she said, "The materials of science are the materials of life itself . . . It is impossible to understand man without understanding his environment."

family could suggest that Marjorie had been briefly married. Carson had never had any children of her own, but she loved her great-nephew. However, the situation was very stressful, and it affected her health.

Carson's spirits, though, were lifted when she was able to buy a plot of land on the Maine coast, to build a summer home. She had been visiting the area for several years, and the thought of having a base there from which she could explore the surrounding nature made her happy.

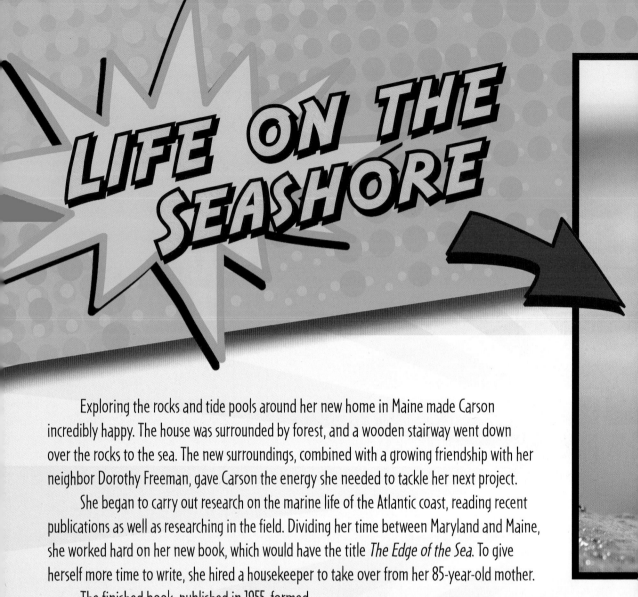

LIFE ON THE SEASHORE

Exploring the rocks and tide pools around her new home in Maine made Carson incredibly happy. The house was surrounded by forest, and a wooden stairway went down over the rocks to the sea. The new surroundings, combined with a growing friendship with her neighbor Dorothy Freeman, gave Carson the energy she needed to tackle her next project.

She began to carry out research on the marine life of the Atlantic coast, reading recent publications as well as researching in the field. Dividing her time between Maryland and Maine, she worked hard on her new book, which would have the title *The Edge of the Sea*. To give herself more time to write, she hired a housekeeper to take over from her 85-year-old mother.

The finished book, published in 1955, formed the third and final part of the sea-life trilogy that Carson had planned years before. It explored the lives of animals in tide pools and elsewhere along the coast, looking at how they exist together in ecosystems. The book got good reviews, sold well,

Carson moved to this house in Maryland with Roger. Raising him was an important part of her life.

A Beloved Adopted Son

Carson never had any of her own children, but when her niece Marjorie died suddenly in 1957, she adopted Marjorie's son, Roger. At the time, he was just five years old. He and his great-aunt became incredibly close.

SUPERHERO FACT

Snap!

The crabs that live in rock pools along the coasts of the world were featured in *The Edge of the Sea*.

and was translated into many other languages. As with *The Sea Around Us*, several chapters were published in magazines, which increased its popularity.

Now that she had finished the ocean trilogy, Carson began to look for a new topic. She planned a book about evolution, but gave up the idea when another scientist published one on the same subject. Instead, she turned her attention to conservation, and started getting involved with groups such as The Nature Conservancy. Maybe, she thought, a book about conservation should be her next project.

NATURE WARRIORS

In Carson's time, concern for the environment was not as widespread as it is today. During the nineteenth century, writers such as Henry David Thoreau had written about nature and its importance. In 1872, Yellowstone in Wyoming had become the first national park in the United States. Then, in 1892, the writer and naturalist John Muir and others founded the Sierra Club, which had the goal of protecting America's natural resources.

In the 1950s, pollution was a real problem. Industry was growing, but there were few controls in place.

However, aside from a small band of dedicated conservationists, there was little else to protect nature. In the first half of the twentieth century, times were hard, and caring for the environment was a luxury few could afford. Factories and industry were growing at an amazing rate, but often at an environmental cost—there were few laws to limit pollution and protect natural resources. Conservation was seen by many people to be an obstacle in the path of progress.

Since childhood, Carson had been interested in nature, and much of her writing focused on the relationship between humans and the natural world. She had always felt that human actions

Pollution Peril

By the 1950s, pollution was finally starting to be seen as a problem with serious consequences—for nature as well as for people's health. In 1948, the government passed the Water Pollution Control Act, followed by the Air Pollution Control Act in 1955. These laws, however, did not give the government any real power to punish polluters. There was still a lot more to do.

SUPERHERO FACT

Henry David Thoreau is best known for *Walden*, a book about living simply in natural surroundings.

could have a devastating effect on nature, and she began research on the subject. However, Carson soon realized that she needed a narrower focus. Back in 1945, her job at the Bureau of Fisheries had brought her into contact with scientists studying the effects of a new pesticide called DDT. She had proposed an article about DDT to the *Reader's Digest* magazine, but it turned her down. Now, more than a decade later, Carson decided it was time to revisit the topic.

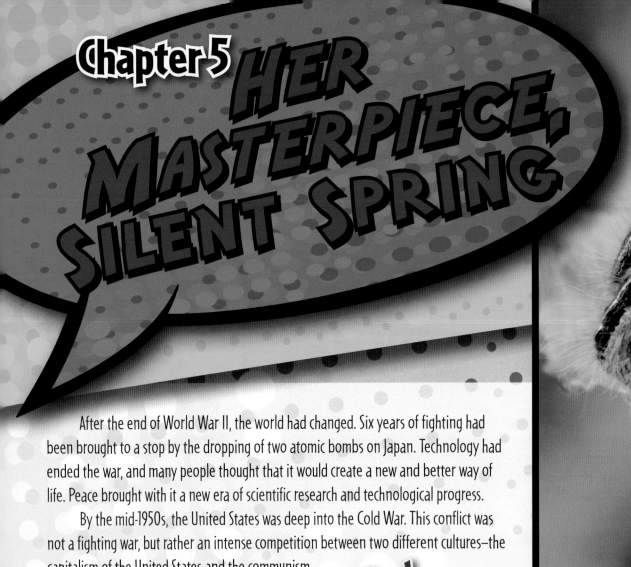

Chapter 5
HER MASTERPIECE, SILENT SPRING

After the end of World War II, the world had changed. Six years of fighting had been brought to a stop by the dropping of two atomic bombs on Japan. Technology had ended the war, and many people thought that it would create a new and better way of life. Peace brought with it a new era of scientific research and technological progress.

By the mid-1950s, the United States was deep into the Cold War. This conflict was not a fighting war, but rather an intense competition between two different cultures—the capitalism of the United States and the communism of the Soviet Union. Each country turned to science to prove that its way was best, and billions of government dollars were pumped into research into space travel, nuclear weapons, and ways to make industry more effective.

Zap!

The caterpillars of the gypsy moth eat leaves in huge numbers. They are one of the pests targeted by synthetic pesticides.

One area of huge growth was chemical pesticides. For as long as people had been farming crops, insects and other tiny living things had been a problem. Sometimes whole harvests could be lost because of infestation. In addition, some of the pests carried

Billions of Pounds of Pesticides

In the 1930s, the total amount of pesticides sprayed in the United States was about 500 million pounds (227 million kg) each year. By the end of World War II, this had almost doubled to just under 1 billion pounds (455 million kg) a year, and during the 1970s around 1.5 billion pounds (680 million kg) of pesticides were sprayed annually, before usage started to decline. In the post-war years, the use of synthetic pesticides such as DDT increased sharply, until restrictions were introduced in 1972.

disease. Farming was a risky business, but many people felt that science could help to eliminate the risk.

In the 1940s and 1950s, aerial spraying of crops with pesticides–known as "crop dusting"– became common. Chemicals such as chlordane, aldrin, and DDT had been developed during the war to help keep soldiers safe from disease. The belief was that spraying such chemicals on crops would not just control the insects–it would wipe them out. The benefits to farmers could be huge. However, no one had studied the long-term effects of these substances in any detail.

PESTICIDE DANGER

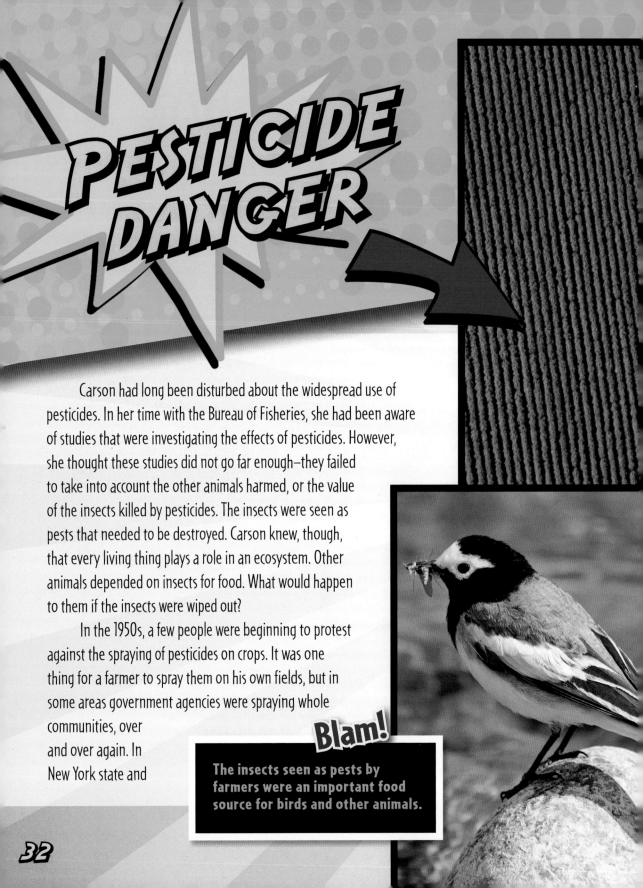

Carson had long been disturbed about the widespread use of pesticides. In her time with the Bureau of Fisheries, she had been aware of studies that were investigating the effects of pesticides. However, she thought these studies did not go far enough—they failed to take into account the other animals harmed, or the value of the insects killed by pesticides. The insects were seen as pests that needed to be destroyed. Carson knew, though, that every living thing plays a role in an ecosystem. Other animals depended on insects for food. What would happen to them if the insects were wiped out?

In the 1950s, a few people were beginning to protest against the spraying of pesticides on crops. It was one thing for a farmer to spray them on his own fields, but in some areas government agencies were spraying whole communities, over and over again. In New York state and

Blam!

The insects seen as pests by farmers were an important food source for birds and other animals.

Pesticide Articles Rejected

Marie Rodell, Carson's agent, tried to get magazines interested in an article on pesticides. However, the New York lawsuit had gone all the way to the Supreme Court, where it was dismissed on a technicality. Because of this, magazine editors were reluctant to publish an article that went against the court's opinion.

SUPERHERO FACT

Spraying crops from an airplane is called crop dusting, and it was first developed in the 1920s. It is an effective way to spread pesticides, fertilizer, or other substances quickly over a large area.

other places people filed lawsuits against the government to keep them from spraying on their backyards. They argued that the pesticides were not just killing mosquitoes—they were harming other wildlife as well, especially birds.

Carson began contacting other scientists to see what they knew about pesticides, as well as talking to some of the residents who had brought one of the lawsuits. Thanks to her contacts in the government, she was able to get copies of several reports on pesticide use. She started to gather and organize a large amount of information. The more she learned, the more committed she became to spreading the word about the dangers of pesticides. Her original idea had been to write a magazine article or two, but now she was planning a book.

FACING CHALLENGES

Carson's research was going slowly, but she was finding a lot of good material. Scientists around the United States had been gathering evidence on how pesticides were affecting wildlife, and Carson began to bring it all together and look for patterns. One strand was the effect on birds–there was evidence that some pesticides caused birds to lay eggs with thinner eggshells, which led to population losses. Another strand of her research focused on insects building up resistance to pesticides. This meant that the pesticides were becoming less effective at killing pests, which led to further crop spraying.

One of Carson's main areas of research was the effect of pesticides on human health. When pesticides were

SUPERHERO FACT

Cranberry Scandal!

Pesticides became big news in 1959. A weed killer–aminotriazole–had been approved for use on cranberry bogs, but only after the berries had been picked. However, some growers used the chemical before harvest, and berries were contaminated. Worse still, studies showed that the chemical could cause cancer. Just before Thanksgiving, the government put out a warning. Supermarkets immediately took the berries off their shelves and many tons were destroyed.

The ban on cranberries caused by pesticides was devastating for fruit farmers.

sprayed on fields and towns, they landed on crops and also seeped into the groundwater. Some chemicals in pesticides could be absorbed directly through the skin. Biologists were investigating the ability of these chemicals to cause cancer in humans as well as animals. Repeated exposure to pesticides allowed the chemicals to build up in a person's body, and the scientists were studying what long-term health effects might result.

In 1958, while Carson was deep into her research, her beloved mother suffered a stroke and died not long afterward. Carson was devastated, but she continued working, despite her own health problems. In early 1960, she had a stomach ulcer, and in April that year she was diagnosed with breast cancer. After surgery to remove the cancer, she continued working. She was determined to finish the book, which she did in 1962.

WHAT IS A "SILENT SPRING"?

It was Marie Rodell who suggested using *Silent Spring* as the title for the book. It refers to the introduction, in which Carson recounts a "fable" about a town feeling the effects of pesticides. She wrote: "The birds, for example–where had they gone? . . . The feeding stations in the backyards were deserted. The few birds seen anywhere were moribund; they trembled violently and could not fly. It was a spring without voices."

Throughout the rest of the book, Carson slowly but surely piled up the evidence against pesticides. She suggested that they should really be called "biocides," because they had an effect on many living things, not just the pests they targeted. They were damaging whole ecosystems and causing pollution in the soil and water. There were also four chapters detailing the effects of pesticides on human health.

One of the examples given in the book was the use of dieldrin in Sheldon, Illinois, where the goal was to eliminate the Japanese beetle. Laboratory tests had shown that dieldrin was 50 times more poisonous to birds

Robins are a traditional sign of spring, but after the pesticide spraying in Sheldon, Illinois, hardly any were left.

Call for Natural Pest Control

In the final chapter of *Silent Spring*, Carson proposed the use of biological pest control. This means using nonchemical methods for controlling harmful insects. For example, farmers could introduce spiders or other natural predators, or create habitats for insect-eating bats.

STAR CONTRIBUTION

In the 1940s and 1950s, DDT was not just used on crops. Here it is being sprayed on sheep in order to kill ticks that spread disease.

than DDT. The pesticide killed the young beetle grubs, but the birds that ate the dying grubs were poisoned too. Many different species in the area were nearly wiped out, and 90 percent of cats in the area died as well.

The book also warned of the other consequences of over-using pesticides. One of these was the idea that insects would gradually become resistant to the chemicals, making the pesticides useless. Carson did not think that pesticides should be completely banned. Instead, she argued that they should be used sparingly when necessary, and always targeted to have the greatest effect.

PUBLICATION AND CONTROVERSY

A storm of publicity greeted the publication of *Silent Spring* in 1962. Even before the book came out, in September, several chapters had been published in *The New Yorker*, an influential magazine. The powerful chemical industry was quick to fight back, worried that Carson's book might lead to a ban on the pesticides that brought it millions of dollars each year.

The criticisms of the book took many forms. Some opponents said that since Carson was a marine biologist, not a chemist, she was not qualified to judge the effects of pesticides. Others claimed—wrongly—that she was calling for a total ban, which could lead to the spread of disease. Some argued that since *Silent Spring* had been written for the general public, scientists should not take it seriously. And many critics attacked Carson personally. She was a fanatical nature-lover, they said, who

SUPERHERO FACT

No Case to Answer

One chemical company, Velsicol, threatened to sue Carson's publisher and the magazines that printed extracts from *Silent Spring*. But *The New Yorker*'s lawyer told them, "Everything in those articles has been checked and is true. Go ahead and sue." Velsicol never did.

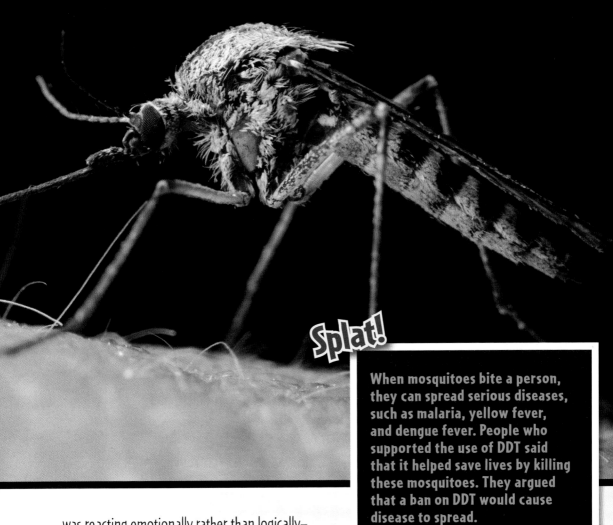

Splat!

When mosquitoes bite a person, they can spread serious diseases, such as malaria, yellow fever, and dengue fever. People who supported the use of DDT said that it helped save lives by killing these mosquitoes. They argued that a ban on DDT would cause disease to spread.

was reacting emotionally rather than logically– probably in part because she was a woman.

However, Carson's book also had its supporters. Her publisher had known that the book would be heavily criticized by the chemical industry, so it had lined up supporters in advance. Earlier, Carson had sent draft chapters of the book to respected scientists for checking. Now these scientists became useful as defenders of her message.

It was good that Carson had such loyal supporters, because she was not up to fighting her attackers. Her cancer had spread throughout her body and she was undergoing radiation treatment, which left her tired and sick. However, she wanted to hide her disease from the public. She would have to give talks and interviews to defend the book, and she wanted the focus to be on *Silent Spring* rather than on her health.

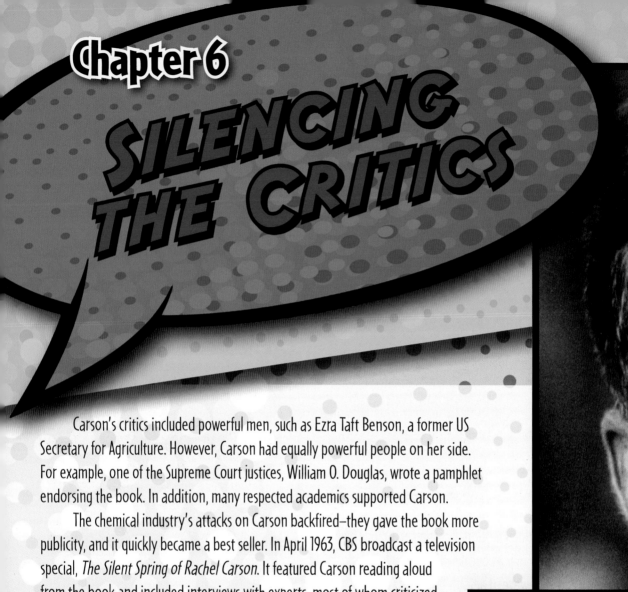

Chapter 6

SILENCING THE CRITICS

Carson's critics included powerful men, such as Ezra Taft Benson, a former US Secretary for Agriculture. However, Carson had equally powerful people on her side. For example, one of the Supreme Court justices, William O. Douglas, wrote a pamphlet endorsing the book. In addition, many respected academics supported Carson.

The chemical industry's attacks on Carson backfired—they gave the book more publicity, and it quickly became a best seller. In April 1963, CBS broadcast a television special, *The Silent Spring of Rachel Carson*. It featured Carson reading aloud from the book and included interviews with experts, most of whom criticized the book. Carson's quiet confidence and knowledge of her subject impressed viewers more than the negative comments of the "experts."

About 15 million people watched the television program, and public opinion began to turn against pesticides. The very next day, Senator Hubert Humphrey announced that he was forming a government committee to review environmental dangers, including pesticides. Carson was asked to testify before the committee. Just a month later, the President's Science

William O. Douglas loved the outdoors and often supported environmental causes.

More Than a Million Sold

After its publication in September 1962, *Silent Spring* spent most of the fall at number one on the best-seller list. By Christmas, it had sold more than 160,000 copies, and in the first two years it sold more than 1 million copies.

Advisory Committee published a long-awaited report on the effects of pesticides. The report admitted that Carson's case against pesticides was strong, and it called for changes in government regulation. President Kennedy released a statement saying that he would think about ways to address the committee's recommendations. Could there be a change in the law on pesticides?

Carson knew she had a real chance to change the way pesticides were used. Despite constant pain from her cancer, she prepared carefully for her appearance in front of the government committees. She knew that she probably did not have long to live, and she wanted to make sure that her work had a positive effect on the world.

Blam!

President Kennedy was determined to act on the suggestions of his Science Advisory Committee.

BATTLING TO THE LAST

In May 1963, Carson traveled to Capitol Hill to testify before the Senate committee. The room was packed to hear her evidence. She talked for nearly an hour as the senators questioned her. With quiet determination, she outlined the damage caused by synthetic pesticides and argued for strict regulations on spraying. It should, she said, be reduced to the minimum strength required, and pesticides with long-lasting residues should be phased out.

Carson found herself showered with awards. The National Council of Women awarded her their first-ever "Woman of Conscience" award. She won both the Audubon Medal and the Cullum Geographical Medal (from the American Geographical Society). She was also inducted into the American Academy of Arts and Letters. However,

SUPERHERO FACT

Protecting Human Rights

In her testimony to the Senate committee, Carson spoke up for "the right of the citizen to be secure in his own home against the intrusion of poisons applied by other persons. I speak not as a lawyer but as a biologist and as a human being, but I strongly feel that this is or should be one of the basic human rights."

Populations of the peregrine falcon declined steeply due to use of DDT but recovered after the pesticide was banned.

her cancer was taking its toll. She had to turn down many invitations to give speeches, but in September–even though she was confined to a wheelchair–she traveled to San Francisco to give a speech called "The Pollution of the Environment." In her speech, she called herself an "ecologist" for the first time.

In January 1964, Carson caught a serious respiratory infection, followed by meningitis. She also had a heart condition. In March, her doctors discovered that the cancer had spread to her liver. Only her closest friends knew how sick she was–she told others that she was suffering from arthritis. Just before sunset on April 14, 1964, Carson died of a heart attack at the age of 56. Her ashes were scattered along the Atlantic coast that she loved so much.

CARSON'S CONSERVATION LEGACY

Carson's work had a huge impact on the environmental movement in the 1960s. Her work brought the issue of pesticides to the country's attention, and communities began to organize on a grassroots level to stop the use of dangerous pesticides. The public began to demand that scientists and the government should take responsibility for the effects of their policies. The Environmental Defense Fund, a nonprofit campaign group, was set up in 1967 to fight against DDT.

Many laws were changed as a result of *Silent Spring*. President Richard Nixon set up the Environmental Protection Agency in 1970. Its mission is to protect human health and the environment by drawing up and enforcing new laws. Before then, the Department of Agriculture was in charge of regulating pesticides as well as promoting agriculture. This was a conflict of interest, because the Department of Agriculture was not responsible for any effects on wildlife.

Throughout the 1970s, new laws were passed to protect the air, water, and human health. For example, the Clean Water Act was passed in 1972, along with a ban on the agricultural use of DDT. In April 1970, the first Earth Day was held, bringing millions of people out to campaign for environmental reform.

Through her talents as a writer and a scientist, Carson changed the way we think about the environment, and how we balance scientific

A wildlife refuge in the Maine wilderness that she loved so much is now named the Rachel Carson National Wildlife Refuge.

Controversy Continues

Not everyone believes that Carson's legacy is a positive one. Some people think that the ban on DDT allowed disease-carrying mosquitoes to spread, causing millions of deaths from malaria around the world. However, most scientists disagree. DDT was only banned for agricultural use—it is still effective when specifically targeted to fight malaria.

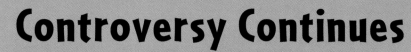
SUPERHERO FACT

progress and conservation. She made people demand accountability from industry and from government, and think about ways to live in harmony with nature. Even though many environmental problems still exist, the world is a very different place, thanks to her work—and most especially her groundbreaking book, *Silent Spring*.

Rachel Carson

USA 17c

Carson was honored with a postage stamp in 1981.

Glossary

accountability accepting responsibility for your own actions

aerial taking place in or from the air

agent someone who works on behalf of another person to help sell their work and make sure they are treated fairly

capitalism an economic system in which land, factories, and other resources are owned by individuals, instead of the government

Cold War the non-violent conflict between the United States and the Soviet Union from the 1950s through the 1980s

communism a political and economic system in which all industry and natural resources are owned by the government, to be shared out in an equal way

conservation the protection of natural resources, such as oceans or forests, from pollution or destruction

contagious able to be passed from one living thing to another when they come into contact

contaminated damaged by being exposed to harmful substances

DDT a type of powerful pesticide, widely used from about 1950 to 1980, mainly for killing mosquitoes and other insects

ecosystem a community of living things, such as plants and animals, and the environment they live in

evolution the process of changing and adapting to an environment over time

field research gathering first-hand information by going out to observe directly, instead of learning from books or doing experiments in a laboratory

genetics the study of traits and how they are passed on from one living thing to its offspring

grassroots originating with ordinary people, who work together to gain support and make changes

habitat the natural environment of an animal or plant

invertebrates animals without a backbone

lawsuits cases brought before a court, when one person or group has a strong complaint against another

magna cum laude the second-highest academic honor given to a person graduating from a college or university

malaria a serious disease, spread by mosquitoes, that causes chills, fever, and sweating

marine biologist someone who studies marine biology–researching plants and animals that live in the sea or on the coasts

natural resources materials that are found in nature and can be used by people–for example coal or trees

pesticides chemical substances used to kill the insects that harm plants and crops

PhD an academic degree, which stands for doctor of philosophy

pollution contaminating something, such as water or air, with harmful substances

predators animals that must kill and eat other animals in order to live

radiation the waves of energy sent out by radioactive material, which can be harmful to health but can also help treat cancer by destroying cancerous cells

resistance an ability to withstand the effects of something, which insects can develop if frequently exposed to pesticides, so that they are no longer harmed by them

synthetic not natural, but made by people instead

testify to give evidence in a court of law or before another official body

tide pools pockets of water from the sea that are left in rocky pools on the beach when the tide goes out

zoology the study of animals

For More Information

Books

Fabiny, Sarah. *Who Was Rachel Carson?* New York, NY: Grosset & Dunlap, 2014.

Hile, Lori. *Rachel Carson: Environmental Pioneer* (Women in Conservation). Chicago, IL: Heinemann Library, 2014.

Levine, Ellen. *Up Close: Rachel Carson.* New York, NY: Puffin, 2008.

Macgillivray, Alex. *Understanding Rachel Carson's Silent Spring* (Words that Changed the World). New York, NY: Rosen Publishing, 2010.

Miller, Marie-Therese. *Rachel Carson* (Conservation Heroes). New York, NY: Chelsea House Publishers, 2011.

Quaratiello, Arlene. *Rachel Carson: A Biography* (Greenwood Biographies). Westport, CT: Greenwood, 2004.

Websites

Find a biography and timeline of Carson's life, as well as information on her books, at:
www.rachelcarson.org

Discover the wildlife refuge named after Rachel Carson in Maine at:
www.fws.gov/refuge/rachel_carson

Learn about the Rachel Carson Council, founded to carry on her work after her death, at:
www.rachelcarsoncouncil.org

For more biographical information on Rachel Carson, see:
www.chatham.edu/rachelcarson/rachelcarson.cfm

For a biography of Carson that talks about her writing, try:
www2.epa.gov/aboutepa/rachel-carson

Publisher's note to educators and parents: Our editors have carefully reviewed these websites to ensure that they are suitable for students. Many websites change frequently, however, and we cannot guarantee that a site's future contents will continue to meet our high standards of quality and educational value. Be advised that students should be closely supervised whenever they access the Internet.

Index